Fingerpower® FUN

Primer Level

Compiled, edited and arranged by Wesley Sch

FOREWORD

The purpose of these pieces is to provide musical experiences beyond the traditional Fingerpower® books. The series offers students fun-to-play melodies which have many technic benefits. The pieces are arranged in order of progressive difficulty and nicely supplement all method books at this level.

A planned variety of rhythms, key signatures, time signatures, dynamics and use of staccato helps develop basic musicianship. Most pieces have the melody divided between hands in five-finger position. Large, widely spaced notes help make music reading easier.

A short technic preparatory drill ("Finger Workout") focuses on some of the melodic patterns found in each piece.

Duet accompaniments offer many possibilities for recital participation. The duets help provide rhythmic training and ensemble experience especially valuable at the early elementary level and are recommended for use at home as well as at the lesson. The student should, however, practice the solo part first, until the notes and rhythm are secure.

INDEX

EXCLUSIVELY DISTRIBUTED BY

HAL•LEONARD®

17-23

2

Finger Workout: Play this exercise five times daily as a warm-up for "Hanging Out."

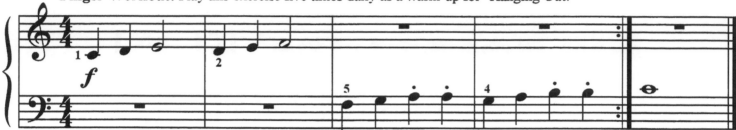

Hanging Out

Andantino ♩ = 100-108

Wesley Schaum

*Duet Accompaniment (Solo part should be played with both hands one octave higher than written.)

* Stem up = R.H. Stem down = L.H.

4

Finger Workout: Play this exercise five times daily as a warm-up for "Short and Sweet."

Short and Sweet

Moderato ♩ = 112-120

Wesley Schaum

Duet Accompaniment (Solo part should be played with both hands one octave higher than written.)

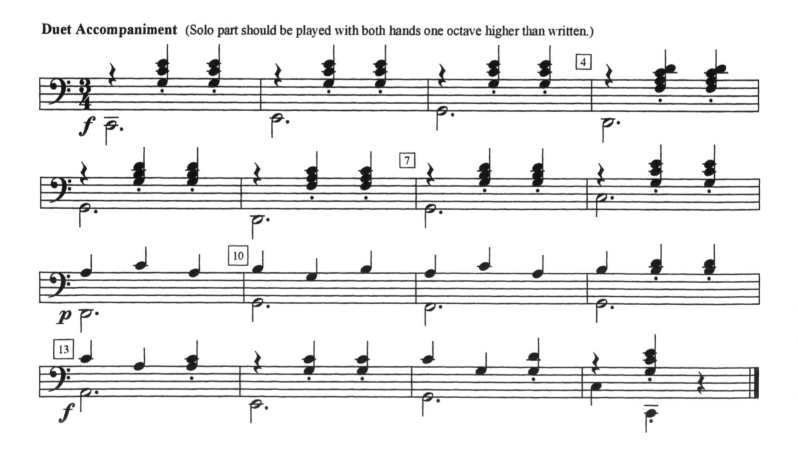

6

Finger Workout: Play this exercise five times daily as a warm-up for "Yankee Doodle."

Yankee Doodle

Vivo ♩= 120-132

Traditional

Duet Accompaniment (Solo part should be played with both hands one octave higher than written.)

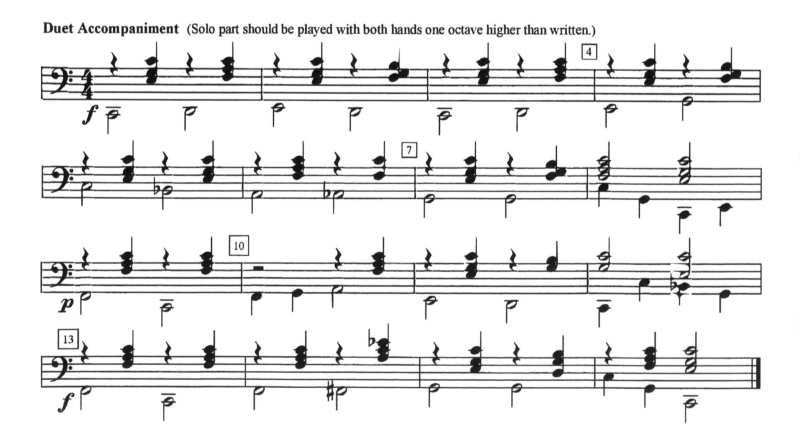

8

Finger Workout: Play this exercise five times daily as a warm-up for "Runaround."

Runaround

Cantabile ♩ = 104-112

Wesley Schaum

Duet Accompaniment (Solo part should be played with both hands one octave higher than written.)

Finger Workout: Play this exercise five times daily as a warm-up for "Chill Out."

Chill Out

Moderato ♩= 112-120

Wesley Schaum

Duet Accompaniment (Solo part should be played with both hands one octave higher than written.)

Finger Workout: Play this exercise five times daily as a warm-up for "Bag of Tricks."

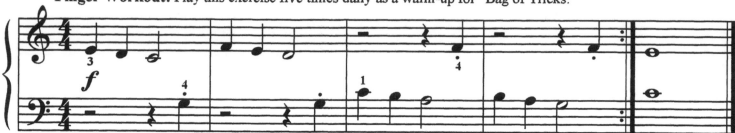

Bag of Tricks

Andantino ♩ = 96-104

Wesley Schaum

Duet Accompaniment (Solo part should be played with both hands one octave higher than written.)

Finger Workout: Play this exercise five times daily as a warm-up for "Little Swinger."

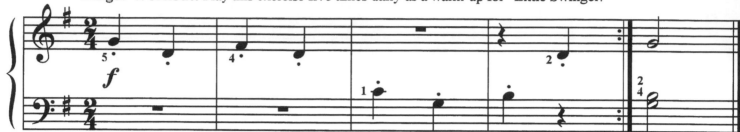

Little Swinger

Giocoso ♩ = 108-116

Wesley Schaum

Duet Accompaniment (Solo part should be played with both hands one octave higher than written.)

Finger Workout: Play this exercise five times daily as a warm-up for "Energized."

Energized

Allegretto ♩= 116-126

Wesley Schaum

Duet Accompaniment (Solo part should be played with both hands one octave higher than written.)

Finger Workout: Play this exercise five times daily as a warm-up for "Having a Ball."

Having a Ball

Andantino ♩= 104-112

Wesley Schaum

Duet Accompaniment (Solo part should be played with both hands one octave higher than written.)

Finger Workout: Play this exercise five times daily as a warm-up for "Big Beat."

Big Beat

Andante ♩= 96-104

Wesley Schaum

Duet Accompaniment (Solo part should be played with both hands one octave higher than written.)

21

Finger Workout: Play this exercise five times daily as a warm-up for "Cool Blues."

Cool Blues

Moderato ♩= 112-120

Wesley Schaum

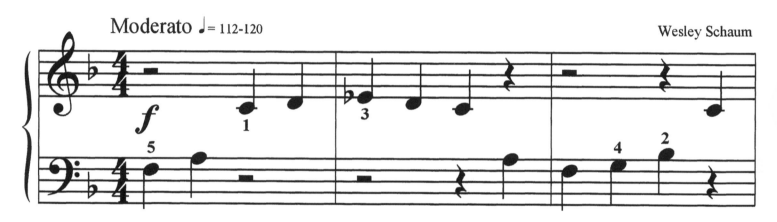

Duet Accompaniment (Solo part should be played with both hands one octave higher than written.)